THE SURPRISING STORY WO**OF** SAM B. WAFFLES WONDER DOG!

Exploring The Surprising Truth Of What We Are!

Written by MT Moonan, Immokalee, Florida, USA

All illustrations and artwork created
By Monique Zuckerman

All rights reserved

A portion of the proceeds from this book will be donated to RCMA—an excellent organization that is making a beautiful difference in the lives of children—an organization that opened their doors to Sam and his friends.

THE SURPRISING STORY WOOF SAM B. WAFFLES WONDER DOG!

First Edition
Book 1 in a 7 Book Series

© 2012 Author MT Moonan, Immokalee, Florida
Graphic Artist, Monique Zuckerman, Bonita Springs, Florida

Printed in the United States of America

Dedicated to Sam B. Waffles, My Teacher (1997-2009)

Sam was always ready for a new adventure!

Sam was a good dog... she will be missed. Sam didn't need much to be happy. A good walk with a friend, time to roll in the grass and a scratch behind her ear was all that was needed. Sam had a way with children. Making big smiles appear on little faces was easy for her... Sam was always kind and always gentle with our children... What more could you want from a friend?

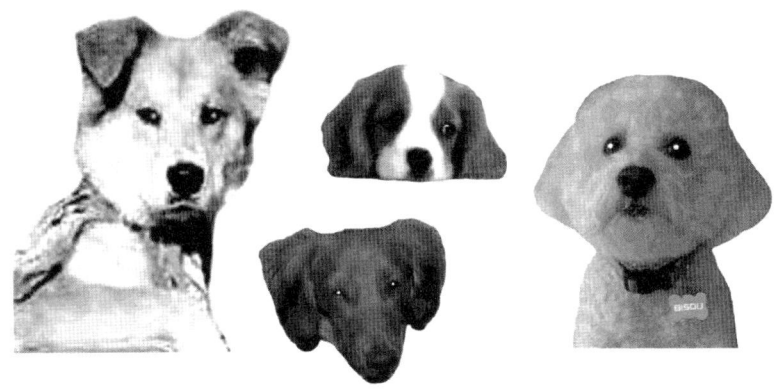

Sam had many important friends!

Special Note

Many quotes in this book are from the wisdom of others…
If there is redeeming value in this book then it came through the author and not from the author.

Reviews

"**The Surprising Story of Sam B. Waffles Wonder Dog grabbed my attention and, two months later; it still won't let me go.**" Jean Eklund, editor of the RCMA HOY

"**The Surprising Story of Sam B. Waffles Wonder Dog is a book for all ages.**" Judy Brill

Introduction

Chapter 1—Sometimes it hurts

Chapter 2—The Healing

Chapter 3—Exploring

Chapter 4—Sometimes a shadow blocks the light!

Chapter 5—Transformation

Chapter 6—Change

Chapter 7—The Challenge

Chapter 8—Inspiration and Forgiveness

Chapter 9—Reflections on friendship

Conclusion—Epilogue

Mandy Update

Lessons from Sam

Contact Information

About the Author

About the Artist

A Life's Mission…

1. Go to the mountains
2. Accept your gifts
3. Develop your gifts
4. Give your gifts away
5. Report back for more gifts!

"When we find a tune in our hearts,
We owe the world a song."
Glenn Cunningham

"The number of seeds in an apple can easily
be counted… The number of apples in a seed…
Now here's an idea to ponder…"
Robert H.Schuller

The greatest things in life are not things…
Anthony J. D'Angelo

And remember, nothing lasts forever!

Story Tellers Rule # 78.4

1. All stories are true.
2. Some of them actually happened.
3. All stories are about you and me—we play all the parts...
                              As told by M. Mckenna

Special Note to Youngsters

Please, never ride with your head out the window. The reason is that you could get bumped and bruised by bugs and trees and hard stuff that cause a lot of hurting. Bugs will stain your teeth and your smile will lose a lot of its face value.

Sam taught me to stick my head out the window only while parked on top of windy hills or on the edge of oceans where big breezes come to visit.

Contributors to this Book

Special thanks to Sam B. Waffles, Monique Zuckerman, Jean, Judy, Cuby and Bert.

This is Sam's good friend Bert* enjoying a day out in nature.

**"A real friend sees the first tear,
Catches the second,
And prevents the third."**
Anonymous

*Excuse the interruption: Bert is Sam's friend. Although Bert wasn't part of the original book Sam had promised Bert that he would be included—so here he is.

I've been watching… and I've come to realize that among us are some uncommon people. These people are different in an advanced sort of way. I watch these people and keep track of their behavior. I think they may be trying to tell us something… something significant. Let me give you an example:

Episode 1

"I hate you… I wish you were dead!" These words were screaming out of a little girl and headed straight for her mother.

That did it—until this last out-burst the mother had remained somewhat calm… at least on the surface. Not now! The child's words must have penetrated to a deep wounded part of the mother—for now a cloud of angry pain cast its shadow over the situation. The mother reacted: Violent, painful spanks from the mother's hand attacked the child. Now in a rage, the mother shrieked at her daughter: "Don't you ever talk to me like that! Don't you know I'm your mother?" Spank… Spank… Spank!

The mother's anger turned to pain and she began to weep. Even more screams erupted from the little one… intense crying filled the room making us all feel uncomfortable. The mother, now red-faced and flushed with embarrassment, dragged her screaming child out the door.

We, who were witnesses, were shaking our heads and muttering to each other: "Oh yes, it's uncomfortable and sad to see such behavior. But, we all agreed that the child got exactly what she deserved."

Episode 2

On a different day at a different time the same thing happened, but in a different way.

An emotional storm was raging inside a child and the effects were bursting out all over the place. Angry, ornery, mean-spirited words were flying out of the child... and they were all aimed at her mother.

"What! Oh no! Not again!" I spoke to myself. "She's going to get a good spanking for that!" But no... not this time... this time it was different. I watched with amazement as the mother dropped to one knee, looked into her child's eyes... and softly said: "It looks like you're having a hard day. It sounds like you're upset about something... do you want to talk about it?"

The child's rage eased and the anger drained away... her voice was calm now. "Yes mommy," the child responded with tears as she shared with her mother the hurt and pain of a difficult day at school. And the mother understood...

"You look like you could use a hug." the mother's arms opened and of course, like a shivering child too long in the cold she ran to and melted into her mother's warm embrace.

We who watched were also warmed by the radiance of the Mother's wisdom and love. We stared at the mother and child as they walked away holding hands... And, shaking our heads, we all agreed: "The child got exactly what she deserved!"

**Wise people remember what it was like
to be small, afraid and confused...
They remember... They know...
And they are free to respond in uncommon ways...**

We can learn a lot from watching. Watch closely... raindrops and roses will teach and help us remember. Watch in silence... rabbits, angels, toddlers, trees, mountains and bubbling creeks have lessons for us.

If we are still… then perfectly appropriate lessons will be seen and understood. We will realize that everyone and everything is teaching us what we need to know… teaching us who we really are…

When we are ready a teacher will come. The teacher could come as a man or a woman. However, be alert, the teacher could also come as a child or maybe even as a Wonder Dog!

This book is about being ready: It's about watching, learning and discovering. It's about being different. It's about seeing… It's about the power of Love to heal—and it's about uncovering and sharing our gifts and most of all—It's about remembering what it's like **to be free!**

    The great treasure that we all seek is neither where we think it is nor what we think it is. The great treasure is found right here, right now… and the treasure is the simple "Joy of Being!"

    We had it once, lost it, and now we return to it and feel and know it again as if for the first time. Now this is what I call a "Great Treasure!"

Sometimes it causes me to wonder!

What if deep within us there was a light so wonderful, so beautiful that we wouldn't trade it for a billion, trillion dollars.

And, what if this light became so bright that it warmed all the cold, dark places within us and gave us a peace and joy that words could not explain—when we uncovered this gift we would know that the only way to keep it would be to give it away…

This is a story about a hurt that is healed and lessons that are learned. It's about discovering what is real…It's a story about you and me…

**The source of the force is within us…
Always and in all ways…**

Chapter 1

Sometimes it hurts…

On the other side of a hill, just outside of town is where I found Sam. He was the shakiest dog I had ever met. Reach out to pet him, and he shivered as if to him a hand meant only pain. Speak to him and he would whimper and crawl away.

"Come here boy, I won't hurt you!" I said trying to calm the pup. But Sam wouldn't come… I guess Sam had heard other voices—voices that he couldn't trust.

"Why is that dog so afraid?" I asked the lady who ran the shelter. "Sam got hurt," she told me. "But don't worry, he will be fine. You see… Sam's a Wonder Dog!"

Oh! No...

**There's a brave place within each of us
Where we are never afraid…
Love takes us to that place!**

"Wonder Dog—she must be joking," I said to myself as I walked away. But something wouldn't let me leave. I turned around once more to look… and a chill crawled on me… Sam's frightened eyes stared at me—and a deep remembering came to me… **I remembered what it was like to be afraid.**

    Yep, Sam came with me that day, but it wasn't easy for either of us. Sam spent his days hiding under couches, chairs and beds. "Come here Sam," I would beg, but he wouldn't come. So I would drag him out and he would stand in front of me trembling and shivering like a baby bird alone in a rain-soaked nest. I tried to get the fear out of Sam, but I didn't know how.

    Sam was a trembling shivering bundle of fur… and then one day the trembling stopped.

Chapter 2

The Healing

It was Mandy the neighbor girl who helped Sam heal. She learned of Sam's arrival and soon was at my door. "Can Sam come out to play?" She would ask each morning. "No Mandy," I replied. "Sam's much too afraid. If you get close to Sam he may think you are trying to hurt him and he may bite you." "May I try?" Mandy asked with kindness in her voice. "Well… I don't know Mandy…" I was ready to say no, but to my surprise I said.

"Well … I guess it would be all right. But be careful," I warned. "You can't trust a dog that's been hurt—a dog that's so full of fear."

As Mandy approached Sam the shaking and whimpering reappeared… he began to growl! But, just as I was ready to stop Mandy, somehow, someway her soft voice and gentle touch reached Sam. She surrounded him with her arms and whispered a message into his ear.

What Mandy said, I don't know, but as Sam stared into her eyes the light of forgotten warmth returned to him, the fear melted away and a mysterious stillness began to emerge.

> **"A wise teacher makes spaces and takes us Places where we can't help but grow"**

Mandy walked with Sam down shady streets and around little lakes. She talked with him under big leafy trees, sharing sweet stories of summers on the farm with grandma and grandpa. She gave Sam lots of hugs and tickled his nose with flowers. Each day she would hug him until all his shivers were squeezed out, and then she would talk in quiet whispers and chase away his fear.

Sam was remembering what it was like to be loved—the trembling stopped and the whimpering went away!

Sam got changed. The warmth of Mandy's presence helped Sam become a different dog. Mandy brought a bounce to Sam's step and his bark began to have a smile in it.

    I was amazed by the sudden change in Sam, and I couldn't help but smile as I watched Mandy and Sam march away like brave souls setting out on a great adventure.

    Mandy and Sam became the best of friends…

**It's hard to be afraid when there's a Big,
Brave Spirit that's always with you!**

Chapter 3

Exploring

Sam became an explorer. He spent hours chasing butterflies and turning over rocks. He dug deep holes, found wiggly worms and strange bugs. He sniffed out smells that filled his nose with tickling surprise! His eyes now opened BIG to see a world of wonder. Sam discovered the kind of stuff that would get a dog truly excited — things like sticks, rocks and porcupines.

Sam found things you just had to share with a friend… and Mandy was that friend for Sam. And being with her made everything more than twice as fun and less than half as hard.

WARNING!

**When in doubt don't wake up grouchy…
Let your dad sleep as long as he wants…**

Special Note

Grouchy, crabby people had to be careful around Mandy and Sam. If naturally negative people got too close they would get sprinkled by the overflow of Mandy's and Sam's splashing joy.

People with frowns couldn't maintain them. Joyful energy would penetrate the grumpy causing frowns to flip and smiles to form. Giggles and chuckles would burst out making eyes water and bellies shake. Sometimes weeks would pass before these effects would fade… and sometimes, the angry annoyance and persistent sadness would disappear—never to return.

A Story Time-Out!

Since I have a Poetic License I am allowed to call a Story Time-Out. Every story teller with a poetic license is given 4 time-outs that can be applied anywhere and at anytime. The time-out can be used to insert off-the-subject advice or tell an amusing off-the-subject story.

Poetic Advice: Stop, be still… Now slowly turn your head until you spot a hugging opportunity. Now, without warning give a mirthful snuggle. In the midst of this unprovoked act of hugging whisper a few words of encouragement:

*"I love the way I feel when I'm with you!"
*"Thanks for being so advanced!"
*"May the Source of the Force Be with you!"
*"Your hugs squeeze the sadness out of me."
*"I like the cut of you jib."
    (This is a good whisper for the nautically inclined)

Please whisper these kind words
or words of higher value.
And remember…

Hugs strengthen the immune system
And reconnect us to our authentic nature.

Extra Special Note

Head Start Centers offer high level hugging opportunities. So if the lonely chills ever sneak up on you quickly go to the nearest Head Start Center. Find a baby, find a rocking chair, gaze into the baby's eyes as you slowly begin to rock and the baby will lead you back to stillness… the place where we all speak the same language… the place that is our home…

Ok, stay centered… now, bring that stillness with you as we return to our story...

Each evening when the sun grew tired and began to sink Mandy and Sam would climb the hill outside of town and wave goodbye.

And as the sun painted their faces with an orange-tinted glow they would thank the sun for sharing so willingly its gifts of light and warmth.

And the light in Sam grew even brighter...

Chapter 4

Sometimes a shadow blocks the light!

Life's funny… Just when it seems everything is going all right, it start to go all wrong… or so it seems...

Growing up sometimes gets us down…

The influence of Mandy opened Sam to a bigger world—he began to feel strong and brave. He found out that ducks and squirrels were afraid of him. Puffed up by this discovery, Sam would chase them up trees and into lakes. Sam felt a cruel sense of power, a sad sort of pleasure, and a prideful sense of prestige.

He started to act like he was "Top Dog!" From a dark corner in Sam's mind there came a shadow. Sam got wild and mean. He got corrupted by this newly found power.

Sam began to give me the worries. He lost his shaking but found a dark part of himself. He became a romping, stomping, cat chasing, mailman biting, trash tipping, growling, biting, chewing terror. Sam even developed a bad case of doggie breath. I was beginning to think the world was better off when Sam was afraid.

**We don't choose to be bad,
We forget what it is like to see...
And the night can get very dark...**

Sam started to hang around a bad pack. They weren't really bad dogs but when they got together an ugly part of each of them would appear—and they got mean—they got ugly—and they forgot who they really were.

Daily the pack would gather to startle paper girls and kids who sold cookies. And, when the pack saw all the fear their actions had caused—they would snicker and brag about how brave and fearsome they were. They chased cars and bikes and ambushed mail carriers. They nipped at joggers causing them to leap with fright. They took pleasure at snarling and sneering, growling and grabbing.

What a pack they had become. It became so bad that my Avon Lady refused to visit and my skin go sore, rough and dry.

A Sad Note

I tried to talk some sense into Sam and the pack. But they just gave me bored looks. They grumbled and mumbled as if to say: "You must be confusing us with dogs who give a woof!"

Later I realized that Sam and the pack were too young to know better and too cool to care.

When you forget who you are…
Sometimes you become something else…

I figured Sam needed some tough-love training… and I thought that I was the guy to do it! "Sit!" I demanded… and Sam would stand. "Down!" I shouted… and Sam was up. "Come!" I insisted… and Sam would go. "Fetch!" I instructed… and Sam would frown.

I was getting flabbergasted, agitated and feeling hostile… And I screamed!

"You ugly mutt!" Instantly Sam's face showed a deep sadness. I saw what my words had done and I asked myself: "Why did I have to say that?"

My angry words hit hard and hurt. "Sorry Sam—sometimes when I don't know what to do… I don't know what to do, so I do what I always did."

An Interesting Aside

Those with wisdom know that at a certain stage some dogs have a strong need to rebel and get noticed. Because of this many dogs put their baseball caps on backwards, wear sunglasses on cloudy days and get tattoos that say "Dogs Rule!" and "Humans, leave us dogs alone!" Other dogs may get territorial and start fights with those who wander too close to their dog stuff. These behaviors cause many to complain, blame and shame.

However, blaming, shaming and complaining, designed to help the unruly get better, increases the tendency for them to get bitter.

**"If you know what the seed needs…
The flower will grow!"**

Chapter 5

Transformation

Then one day it happened!

The pack had chased down and cornered a young rabbit. The dogs were closing in, ready to do some serious harm. Sam was right up front with the mean ones. He watched the rabbit with pleasure as it shivered with fright. It looked real bad for the rabbit.

But, something strange began to happen…Sam was shaking!

When you look closely at anyone
You will see yourself!

...Reflected in the rabbits eyes Sam began to see himself. He stared at his image and shivered.

Sam was remembering what it was like to be abused, to be alone, and to be afraid.

A tear formed… change was happening… Sam knew, without a doubt, what he had to do—and he did it!

Special Note

**Bullies can sometimes tell when we're afraid…
And they always know when we're not!**

**You can never tell how far the effects of
a Big Brave Spirit will travel…**

No! Sam barked to the other dogs as he leaped ahead covering the trembling rabbit with his body. The pack stared at Sam in disbelief. "What's going on, we're just having a little fun." They growled at Sam.

Sam stood firm and slowly shook his head from side-to-side. **"No More!"** he yelped. The dog pack didn't know what to do.

Mumbling and grumbling the pack challenged Sam. "No!" Sam barked even more fiercely.

The packed sensed Sam's courage and they got confused and fuzzy-headed. "Go," Sam barked… and slowly, one-by-one they walked away.

Chapter 6

Change

Mandy moved to another town. I was surprised that Sam didn't seem to mind. It was as if somehow Mandy and Sam were still together... as if they were connected to each other in ways I didn't understand.

Sam never again would forget Mandy's influence. However, it turned out that I did.

Sam was becoming famous around the neighborhood. He was getting a lot of attention. However, instead of being happy for Sam I felt jealous. Isn't that strange?

I guess that's why I started to grab the spot light. I told about how Sam was hurt and afraid and how I helped him heal and become brave. I told people about how I taught Sam to explore and discover, but somehow I forgot to tell about Mandy. Sometimes I would get so carried away that I'd tell people things that never even happened... Imagine that!

Later I realized that I had unresolved abandonment and esteem issues. Because of these I sometimes over-tooted my own horn and got stuck playing the same note: me, me, me...

Sam was patient and helped me get back in balance. He helped me recover the part of myself that was Real... A part that didn't need to show off or speak up... a part that is really good to be.

> **Real is something that happens to us...**
> **It usually doesn't happen overnight,**
> **It happens bit-by-bit...**
> The Velveteen Rabbit

Chapter 7

The Challenge

A Wonder Dog can't be ugly!

"You ugly mutt, get the _____ out of here before I kick you." It was tough, mean man who was yelling at Sam.

I could feel my insides get angry. "How dare he yell at my dog that way!" I was mumbling to myself and my blood was starting to boil. Hot, stinging words were churning inside my head ready to explode out of me…

In the middle of all this turmoil Sam began to slowly walk towards the man.

**When you're a Wonder Dog
You know what to do…**

Oh, no," someone in a gathering crowd spoke. "The guy's going to kick the dog!"

The man saw Sam coming. He pulled back his foot readying it to smack Sam.

Ignoring the danger, Sam continued his approach and then, just when things were looking real bad, Sam sat down right in front of the big, burly man. Sam looked up at the man and wagged his tail.

Sam's look was so kind and gentle that everyone couldn't help but feel tingling warmth.

And then... Sam offered the man his paw...

The man looked down at Sam unsure of what to do. But gradually, Sam's message reached the man.

A smile spread across his face—Sam had touched his heart.

"Well ain't that something," the man responded. He gently held Sam's paw and scratched Sam behind the ear. They became friends. The man turned to me and spoke: "You've got a great dog mister!"

I looked at the man and then looked at Sam. I smiled and wondered to myself: "Where did all my upset and anger go?"

We watched the man leave. He was laughing and singing a song about being six days on the road… and that he was going to make it home tonight.

There's no right way to say the wrong thing!

Chapter 8

Inspiration and Forgiveness

You can never overestimate the Influence of advanced behavior...

I was inspired by Sam's action. On the way home I stopped to help an older couple change a flat tire. I picked up 14 pieces of trash and left fifty dollars at the food bank. And, when I got home I called my mother.

"Thanks," I said to Sam as I petted the bundle of fur curled up at my side. It felt good to have a friend with the wisdom and courage to act in such uncommon ways...

*For a Wonder Dog, Emotions are servants, Not Masters

    Yelp, ouch, yikes, yowie!… Oops, I stepped on Sam's tail, "Sorry Sam…" I know it must have hurt—yet Sam never holds a grudge. I guess when you're a Wonder Dog you understand in a deeper and wider way that we're all doing the best that we can.

"Stored hurt, pain, and anger Hurts the container"

Chapter 9

Reflections on friendship

Sam's my friend. We walk over logs and up grassy hills together. We share important stuff like how to find good fetching sticks and quiet places to watch fire flies dance in the dark.

Sometimes we lie together on the sunny side of mountains and watch puffy clouds parade across the sky.

During moments when the timeless truth appears we sit alone together and do some serious non-thinking about empty spaces and deep mysteries.

At night we dream about warm spots on the sunny side of hills, and we imagine the gift of cooling shade on hot summer days.

Sometimes, in-between thoughts, we can see past the edge of forever… and we get goose bumps and we shiver with delight as we imagine about the great adventures that are ready to appear.

I must go now. Sam has a meeting with a caterpillar support group. The group meets weekly to discuss Big Ideas and share dreams of flying.

This may surprise you most caterpillars are clueless about all the exciting changes that they are destined to experience.

Note

Sam has discovered that many caterpillars are discouraged and fearful. The ones walking around all day in the dirt and dust are feeling low. They are disheartened because they think they are stuck living a low level life. The ones in cocoons are terror-stricken, they sense a big change and are frightened that they are about to lose their homes.

Because of these fearful stories Sam has started a caterpillar outreach program. Sam reminds discouraged caterpillars that there's something fresh and exciting ready to be born. And to those snug and comfortable in their cocoons Sam challenges: "Yes, you are safe in your cocoons… but that's not why you were born…

"You were meant to fly!"

Conclusion- Epilogue

Updating what happened to the pack…

Something unexpected happened to the pack that day when Sam said "No!" The pack got influenced by Sam's courage. They got transformed. Little lights came on in their minds. German Shepherds began to reflect, Poodles started to ponder and Rottweiler's began to remember. Hurting, harming and harassing no longer brought the dogs pleasure. They knew that they were made for something better.

They became truly dedicated and highly motivated. The dogs with sharp eyes learned to help the blind. The ones with a keen sense of smell got jobs finding lost children.

Three of the dogs, Max, Bert and Spot went to a shelter for troubled humans and befriended a lonely man named Wally. They took Wally on walks and sat with him under trees—and Wally began to smile. The dogs taught Wally to throw Frisbees. They took turns leaping and snatching the disc in mid-flight.

When Wally got tired Max, Bert and Spot would lead him to cool places to rest. They would surround Wally with their furry bodies and watch him attentively with their big, brown eyes. And when the dogs snuggled close to Wally little tears would form in his eyes—Wally began to remember what it was like to love and be loved.

Wally, Max, Bert and Spot got so good at tossing and catching that they decided to form an act: Wally and His Wonder Dogs! They traveled the country amazing people with their talent.

They touched hearts, helped spirits soar and tickled sensibilities. They visited schools and nursing homes. After each show Wally would share the lessons the dogs had taught him— lessons about healing and growing—lessons about exploring and uncovering—and lessons about courage and doing what needs to be done. In the evening Wally and the Wonder Dogs would sit together to share stories and remember—and when they talked about courage and caring… they always talked about Sam!

Mandy Update...

Mandy moved to Immokalee, Florida and got a job with *RCMA. She became a Head Start Teacher. In her spare time she was an adjunct faculty member at the local community college.

Mandy taught courses in Philosophy, Child Care and Quantum Mechanics.

She also played point guard for the "Wise Guys"— a basketball team that played Tuesday and Thursday nights at the local gym.— and every year she lead the league in assists.

*RCMA is an organization dedicated to opening doors to opportunities for children, parents and staff. At RCMA all the women are advanced and all the men are good-looking.

Lessons from Sam

*Sometimes it hurts

*Every moment has a lesson and a blessing

*Pay attention, learn the lesson, accept the blessing

*There's a Big Brave Spirit in each of us

*There's a place where we all speak the same language

*When we are ready a teacher will come

*Growing up can sometimes get us down

*Remember when you were afraid

*Remember when you were not afraid

*Only the weak are cruel… only the hurt, hurt

*When you're a Wonder Dog, you can't be ugly

*There's a part of us that is never afraid

*It's hard to find the darkness when we bring the light!

*Warning: Non-Judgment Day is near

*Warning: Non-Resistance Day is coming

*For a Wonder Dog emotions are servants, Not Masters

About The Author

Mt Moonan

MT started life centered and with a deep sense of oneness. He spent much time in stillness… then at 6 or 7 or 8 years-of age he began to lose his balance… he fell from grace and became lost in the world of thought… He spent years wandering, trying to return to a centered, balanced life… He went to Reno, Chicago, Fargo, Minnesota, Delhi, Kabul and Ybor City and he still couldn't find what he was looking for. Then he met Sam! MT is still perplexed and confused but now it's about more important things and now it's at a deeper and higher level.

Comments, questions and requests for speaking engagements,
Please contact: mtmoonan@gmail.com

About The Artist

Freelance Graphic Artist, **Monique Zuckerman** comes from the beautiful French Riviera. She has lived in France, North Africa, California and Florida. A true artist in her soul, she developed her passion for drawing when she was a small girl. Over the years Monique has developed her skills in many mediums, including: oil, acrylic, mixed media and illustration. Monique's inspiration comes from her appreciation of the beauty of nature, the landscapes in Provence, the simplicity of life around her, and her deeply held faith. She uses rich, expressive, vibrant colors, which are also a testament to her enthusiasm and love of life.

Monique holds a degree in Graphic Design and Computer Graphics from Platt College Graphic Design School San Francisco California. She held exhibitions of her work in France, California, New Jersey and Florida.

Do you have a book that needs illustrations or artwork? Then you are welcomed to contact Monique.

Contact information: mzuckerman8@hotmail.com

Special Note

Sam: Short for Samuel ("Messenger of God")
Wonder Dog: A dog that has awakened to the excitement, amazement, miraculous, awesome mystery of the Authentic World.

Special Thanks to Sam B. Waffles
For Being so Advanced!

Proof

Made in the USA
Charleston, SC
22 May 2012